£5.25

Welcome to the second Official FA Premier League Annual from Grandreams. Your response to last year's edition was fantastic and we thank you for all your letters and comments. This year we are giving more space to features on the clubs and the star players. There's a month-by-month review of last season's exciting Premiership action and a special feature on our Youth Development Scheme.

You'll also find lots of useful information in the two-part Premiership Club Directory – including the names of each club's Youth Development Officer.

We hope you enjoy reading this Annual, and we hope you will continue to enjoy watching and playing football.

RICK PARRY
Chief Executive
FA Premier League

DON'T
forget to
enter the
brilliant
PREMIERSHIP
COMPETITION

CONTENTS

© The F.A. Premier League 1995

Written and compiled by Tony Lynch
Photographs by Action Images
Designed by Joanna Davies and Louise Ivimy
Thanks to Rick Parry, Adrian Cooke, Nicola Denham and Richard
Carpenter of the FA Premier League
All facts believed correct at time of going to press

Published by Grandreams Ltd, Jadwin House 205–211
Kentish Town Road, London NW5 2JU
Printed in Italy

THE F.A. CARLING PREMIERSHIP

Last season 11,213,168 people passed through the turnstiles of the Premiership stadia – an improvement of 568,617 on the total attendance for 1993–94. And what superb entertainment they had – from Liverpool's 6–1 drubbing of Crystal Palace on the opening day of the season, to the exciting race for the title between Blackburn Rovers and Manchester United on the last day.

That brilliant finish to the 1994–95 campaign confirmed just what a superb competition the Carling Premiership is and why our league is the envy of the world.

And the success story continues. The fourth Carling Premiership season – streamlined to just twenty clubs – is now well under way and has already produced some great games.

......IT'S THE BEST LEAGUE IN THE WORLD!

This season the clubs finishing in the bottom three places in the Carling Premiership table will be relegated to the First Division. The First division champions and runners-up will receive automatic promotion to the Premiership. The third promotion place will go to the winners of the 1995–96 Play-Off final.

The Carling Premiership trophy – the greatest prize in English football

FOCUS ON YOUTH

o become a professional footballer is the great ambition of many youngsters. But just how do you get noticed by the clubs?

'Don't worry,' says Dave Richardson, the Premiership's Director of Youth. 'If a boy is of any quality now at any level of soccer - be it junior league, Sunday league or school football - the clubs will find out about him. Wherever a promising boy is playing his soccer, providing he is working hard and improving his game, there is every chance that he'll get noticed.'

Dave, a vastly experienced Youth Development Officer (formerly with Aston Villa and Leicester City), was appointed by the Premier League last year to co-ordinate improvements in the youth development system, including the gradual transfer of responsibility for youth coaching from the schools to the clubs themselves.

'We know the importance of having a structured Youth Development programme within the Premiership,' says Dave. 'And I am working very closely with the FA through the Programme of Excellence, with the Football League, the PFA, the Managers' Association, the Managerial Staffs Association - and with the English Schools Football Association. Hopefully, with all the Youth Development Officers working hand-in-hand, we'll improve the system for developing our promising 9-16 year-olds.'

Indeed, a successful youth policy goes hand-in-hand with good purchasing on the transfer market. A prime example of this was seen at Manchester United last season, when three or four players who had come up through the Old Trafford system became prominent alongside the big names in the first team. This is an indication of the importance United pay to youth development. Another example is at Liverpool, where Robbie Fowler and Steve McManaman are now key players in Roy Evans' squad - both are products of youth development.

Dave stresses the new emphasis on practice as

Three of Manchester United's rising young stars - David Beckham, Nicky Butt and Simon Davies - they are all products of United's Youth Development programme

opposed to playing lots of games. 'We are taking the lead on this,' he says. 'We need to increase the time spent learning the techniques and skills of the game. Traditionally we've tended to play hundreds of games a year and have just two or three practice sessions - and then we wonder why we're not as technically proficient as other countries!'

Another improvement is an increase in the time that clubs are allowed for Youth Development. 'We used to be restricted to an hour a week, plus a game, with the boys,' says Dave. 'Now we've got unlimited time, which is the right way to proceed. Eventually we should have three or four sessions of technical work per week. Of course, our footballers do have many fine attributes, and we don't want to lose that - we want to add to it. We want to get a better balance.'

Dave is keen to dispel the myth that outstanding schoolboy footballers are the ones who always make the grade. 'Don't be put off if you are not a "star turn" right now,' he says. 'Many key names in football weren't necessarily outstanding schoolboy players - Alan Shearer, Stan Collymore, Andy Cole, Paul Gascoigne, Gary Lineker and Bryan Robson are a few examples.

'Obviously they were all decent schoolboy footballers, but in their age group at 13 and 16 years-old there were other more outstanding players who made their names earlier. Each of those star names had to work extremely hard on their game to develop into top flight players. Believe me, there are some boys playing now who haven't yet been noticed. They will develop slowly then burst onto the scene.

'Opportunity is the key to successful Youth Development, and the Premiership is keen to provide that opportunity.'

Arsenal Stadium, Highbury, London, N5 1BU. Telephone: 0171-226 0304. Ticket Information: 0171-359 0131
Chairman: P.D. Hill-Wood
Manager: Bruce Rioch
Youth Development Officer: T. Murphy
Sponsors: JVC
Nickname: 'The Gunners'
Colours: Red shirts/white sleeves, white shorts, red socks
2nd strip: Navy and teal shirts, navy shorts, navy/teal hooped socks
Pitch size: 110 x 73 yards
Ground Capacity: 40,000

HONOURS
League Champions: 1930–31, 1932–33, 1933–34, 1934–35, 1937–38, 1947–48, 1952–53, 1970–71, 1988–89, 1990–91 (10)
FA Cup Winners: 1930, 1936, 1950, 1971, 1979, 1993 (6)
League Cup Winners: 1987, 1993 (2)
Charity Shield Winners: 1930, 1931, 1933, 1934, 1938, 1948, 1953, 1991 – shared (8)
European Cup-Winners' Cup Winners: 1994 (1)
UEFA Cup Winners: 1970 (1)

PREMIERSHIP PERFORMANCE 1994–95

P	W	D	L	F	A	GD	Pts	Pos
42	13	12	17	52	49	+3	51	12th

Leading Scorer: Ian Wright (18)
Highest Attendance: 38,377

ARSENAL

ASTON VILLA

Villa Park, Birmingham, B6 6HE. Telephone: 0121-327 2299. Ticket Information: 0898 121848 Fax: 0121-322 2107
Chairman: H.D. Ellis
Manager: Brian Little
Youth Development Officer: C. Clarke
Sponsors: AST Computers
Nickname: 'The Villans'
Colours: Claret shirts with claret and blue trim, white shorts, white and claret socks
2nd strip: Green, black and red striped shirts, black shorts, black socks
Pitch size: 115 x 75 yards
Ground Capacity: 46,000

HONOURS
League Champions: 1893–94, 1895–96, 1896–97, 1898–99, 1899–1900, 1909–10, 1980–81 (7)
FA Cup Winners: 1887, 1895, 1897, 1905, 1913, 1920, 1957 (7)
League Cup Winners: 1961, 1975, 1977, 1994 (4)
Charity Shield Winners: 1981 – shared (1)
European Cup Winners: 1982 (1)
European Super Cup Winners: 1982 (1)

PREMIERSHIP PERFORMANCE 1994–95

P	W	D	L	F	A	GD	Pts	Pos
42	11	15	16	51	56	-5	48	18th

Leading Scorer: Dean Saunders (15)
Highest Attendance: 40,154

BLACKBURN ROVERS

Ewood Park, Blackburn, BB2 4JF. Telephone: 01254 698888. Fax: 01254 671042. Ticket information: 0891 121014.
Chairman: R.D. Coar B.Sc
Manager: Kenny Dalglish
Youth Development Officer: J Furnell
Sponsors: McEwans Lager
Nickname: 'Rovers'
Team Colours: Royal blue and white halved shirts, white shorts, blue socks with white trim
Change Colours: Red and black striped shirts, red shorts, black socks
Pitch size: 115 x 72 yards
Ground Capacity: 30,000

HONOURS
League Champions: 1911–12, 1913–14, 1994–95 (3)
FA Cup Winners: 1884, 1885, 1886, 1890, 1891, 1928 (6)
Charity Shield Winners: 1912 (1)

PREMIERSHIP PERFORMANCE 1994–95

P	W	D	L	F	A	GD	Pts	Pos
42	27	8	7	80	39	+41	89	1st

Leading Scorer: Alan Shearer (34)
Highest Attendance: 30,545

Burnden Park, Bolton, BL3 2QR. Telephone: 01204 389200. Fax: 01204 382334 .
Chairman: G. Hargreaves
Manager: Roy McFarland
Youth Development Officer: J. Dewsnip
Sponsors: Reebok
Nickname: 'The Trotters'
Colours: White shirts, navy blue shorts, red socks with blue/white trim
2nd strip: Red and blue striped shirts, white shorts, red socks
Pitch size: 113 x 76 yards
Ground Capacity: 22,500

HONOURS
FA Cup Winners: 1923, 1926, 1929, 1958 (4)

FIRST DIVISION PERFORMANCE 1994–95

P	W	D	L	F	A	GD	Pts	Pos
46	21	14	11	67	45	+22	77	3rd

Leading Scorer: John McGinlay (16)
Highest Attendance: 18,370

BOLTON WANDERERS

Bolton were promoted via the First Division Play-Off Final, beating Reading 4-3 at Wembley.

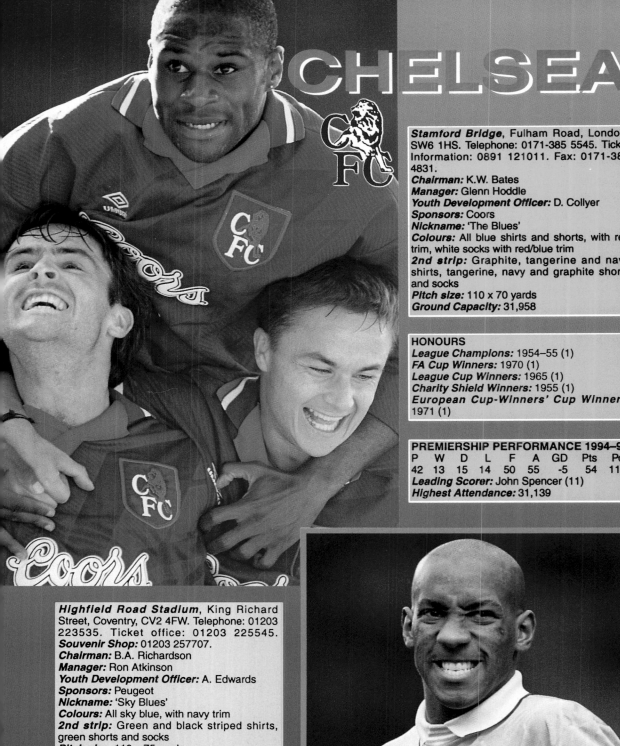

CHELSEA

Stamford Bridge, Fulham Road, London, SW6 1HS. Telephone: 0171-385 5545. Ticket Information: 0891 121011. Fax: 0171-381 4831.
Chairman: K.W. Bates
Manager: Glenn Hoddle
Youth Development Officer: D. Collyer
Sponsors: Coors
Nickname: 'The Blues'
Colours: All blue shirts and shorts, with red trim, white socks with red/blue trim
2nd strip: Graphite, tangerine and navy shirts, tangerine, navy and graphite shorts and socks
Pitch size: 110 x 70 yards
Ground Capacity: 31,958

HONOURS
League Champions: 1954–55 (1)
FA Cup Winners: 1970 (1)
League Cup Winners: 1965 (1)
Charity Shield Winners: 1955 (1)
European Cup-Winners' Cup Winners: 1971 (1)

PREMIERSHIP PERFORMANCE 1994–95

P	W	D	L	F	A	GD	Pts	Pos
42	13	15	14	50	55	-5	54	11th

Leading Scorer: John Spencer (11)
Highest Attendance: 31,139

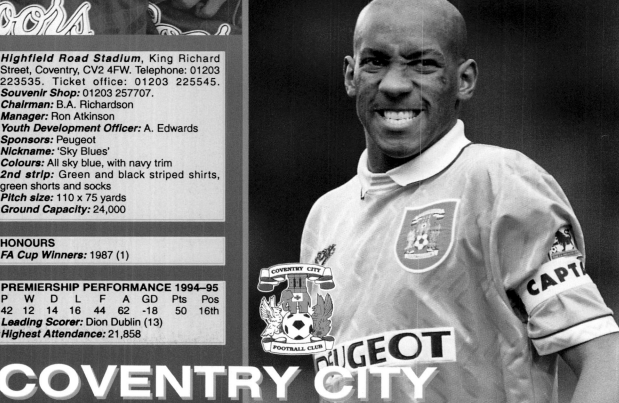

Highfield Road Stadium, King Richard Street, Coventry, CV2 4FW. Telephone: 01203 223535. Ticket office: 01203 225545.
Souvenir Shop: 01203 257707.
Chairman: B.A. Richardson
Manager: Ron Atkinson
Youth Development Officer: A. Edwards
Sponsors: Peugeot
Nickname: 'Sky Blues'
Colours: All sky blue, with navy trim
2nd strip: Green and black striped shirts, green shorts and socks
Pitch size: 110 x 75 yards
Ground Capacity: 24,000

HONOURS
FA Cup Winners: 1987 (1)

PREMIERSHIP PERFORMANCE 1994–95

P	W	D	L	F	A	GD	Pts	Pos
42	12	14	16	44	62	-18	50	16th

Leading Scorer: Dion Dublin (13)
Highest Attendance: 21,858

COVENTRY CITY

EVERTON

Goodison Park, Liverpool, L4 4EL.
Telephone: 0151-521 2020. Fax: 0151-523 9666.
Chairman: Dr. D. M. Marsh
Manager: Joe Royle
Youth Development Officer: R. Hall
Sponsors: NEC
Nickname: 'The Toffees'
Colours: Royal blue shirts, white shorts, white socks
2nd strip: White and grey shirts with black collar, black shorts and socks
Pitch size: 112 x 78 yards
Ground Capacity: 40,500

HONOURS
League Champions: 1890–91, 1914–15, 1927–28, 1931–32, 1938–39, 1962–63, 1969–70, 1984–85, 1986–87 (9)
FA Cup Winners: 1906, 1933, 1966, 1984, 1995 (5)
Charity Shield Winners: 1928, 1932, 1963, 1970, 1984, 1985, 1986 – shared, 1987 (8)
European Cup-Winners' Cup Winners: 1985 (1)

PREMIERSHIP PERFORMANCE 1994–95

P	W	D	L	F	A	GD	Pts	Pos
42	11	17	14	44	51	-7	50	15th

Leading Scorer: Paul Rideout (14)
Highest Attendance: 40,011

LEEDS UNITED

Elland Road, Leeds, LS11 0ES. Telephone: 01532 716037. Ticket Information: 0891 121680. Fax: 01532 720370.
Chairman: L.H. Silver OBE
Manager: Howard Wilkinson
Youth Development Officer: E. Beaglehole
Sponsors: Thistle Hotels
Nickname: 'United'
Colours: All white with blue/yellow trim
2nd strip: Green and blue striped shirts, blue shorts, green socks
Pitch size: 110 x 72 yards
Ground Capacity: 40,000

HONOURS
League Champions: 1968–69, 1973–74, 1991–92 (3)
FA Cup Winners: 1972 (1)
League Cup Winners: 1968 (1)
Charity Shield Winners: 1969, 1992 (2)
UEFA Cup Winners: 1968, 1971 (2)

PREMIERSHIP PERFORMANCE 1994–95

P	W	D	L	F	A	GD	Pts	Pos
42	20	13	9	59	38	+21	73	5th

Leading Scorer: Tony Yeboah (13)
Highest Attendance: 39,426

LIVERPOOL

HONOURS
League Champions: 1900–01, 1905–06, 1921–22, 1922–23, 1946–47, 1963–64, 1965–66, 1972–73, 1975–76, 1976–77, 1978–79, 1979–80, 1981–82, 1982–83, 1983–84, 1985–86, 1987–88, 1989–90 (18)
FA Cup Winners: 1965, 1974, 1986, 1989, 1992 (5)
League Cup Winners: 1981, 1982, 1983, 1984, 1995 (5)
Charity Shield Winners: 1964 – shared, 1965 – shared, 1966, 1974, 1976, 1977 – shared, 1979, 1980, 1982, 1986 – shared, 1988, 1989, 1990 (13)
European Cup Winners: 1977, 1978, 1981, 1984 (4)
UEFA Cup Winners: 1973, 1976 (2)
European Super Cup Winners: 1977 (1)

Anfield Road, Liverpool, L4 0TH. Telephone: 0151-263 2361. Fax: 0151-260 8813.
Chairman: D.R. Moores
Manager: Roy Evans
Youth Development Officer: S. Heighway
Sponsors: Carlsberg
Nickname: 'The Reds'
Colours: All red with white trim
2nd strip: White shirts with green sleeves/black trim, black shorts/white trim, black and green socks with white hoops
Pitch size: 110 x 75 yards
Ground Capacity: 40,500

PREMIERSHIP PERFORMANCE 1994–95

P	W	D	L	F	A	GD	Pts	Pos
42	21	11	10	65	37	+28	74	4th

Leading Scorer: Robbie Fowler (25)
Highest Attendance: 40,014

Maine Road, Moss Side, Manchester, M14 7WN. Telephone: 0161-226 1191/2. Ticket Information: 0891 121591. Fax: 0161-227 9418.
Chairman: F.H. Lee
Manager: –
Youth Development Officers: T. Farrell & C. Bell
Sponsors: Brother
Nickname: 'The Citizens'
Colours: Sky blue shirts with navy trim, white shorts with navy/sky blue trim, sky blue socks with white/navy tops
2nd strip: Red and black striped shirts, black shorts, black socks
Pitch size: 117 x 75 yards
Ground Capacity: 32,000

HONOURS
League Champions: 1936–37, 1967–68 (2)
FA Cup Winners: 1904, 1934, 1956, 1969 (4)
League Cup Winners: 1970, 1976 (2)
Charity Shield Winners: 1937, 1968, 1972 (3)
European Cup-Winners' Cup Winners: 1970 (1)

PREMIERSHIP PERFORMANCE 1994–95

P	W	D	L	F	A	GD	Pts	Pos
42	12	13	17	53	64	-11	49	17th

Leading Scorer: Uwe Rosler (15)
Highest Attendance: 27,850

MANCHESTER CITY

SOCCER
ON THE BOX

There's always soccer on the box as our friends at Sky TV continue to provide unrivalled coverage of Carling Premiership action on Sundays and Mondays – and sometimes on other days too. Every game is covered and viewers need not miss a single goal.

The Sky service also includes regular updates on the Premiership scene via its excellent soccer 'magazine' programmes.

And of course the BBC's long-established Match of the Day remains a constant Saturday night fixture.

1994-95 DIARY OF THE SEASON

AUGUST-
SATURDAY 20th
The third Premier League campaign kicks-off at 3pm precisely. Liverpool are the star turns of the day with a crushing 6-1 away defeat of newly-promoted Crystal Palace. Steve McManaman and Ian Rush score two each and the remaining Reds' goals come from Jan Molby and Robbie Fowler. Tottenham - due to have six points deducted at the end of the season - turn on the style with a 4-3 victory over Sheffield Wednesday at Hillsborough. Germany's star striker Jurgen Klinsmann is on target for Spurs in the 82nd minute - but he is carried off just four minutes later after a clash of heads with Des Walker. Other victories are recorded by Arsenal, Chelsea, Forest and reigning champions Manchester United.

SUNDAY 21st
Kevin Keegan's Newcastle begin their Premiership campaign in real style, with a 3-1 win over newcomers Leicester City at Filbert Street. Andy Cole, top scorer of 1993-94, opens the Magpies' account in the 51st minute. Peter Beardsley and Robbie Elliot add to the scoreline and Julian Joachim pulls one back for Leicester in the last minute.

MONDAY 22nd
Nottingham Forest and Manchester United share the points in a 1-1 draw at the City Ground. Stan Collymore for Forest, and Andrei Kanchelskis for United, are the target men.

TUESDAY 23rd
Leicester are already finding the Premiership tough going. At Ewood Park they lose 3-0 to Kenny Dalglish's polished Blackburn. £5-million-pound man Chris Sutton scores his first goal for Rovers. Henning Berg and Alan Shearer are also on target. Leeds beat Arsenal 1-0, against the run of the play. Wimbledon and Ipswich draw 1-1.

SATURDAY 27th
A great day for goalscorers. At Ewood Park Chris Sutton hits a hat-trick for Blackburn as they lash Coventry 4-0. Paul Walsh and Uwe Rosler score two each as Manchester City trounce

Everton 4-0 at Maine Road. Andy Cole and Steve Watson get two each in Newcastle's 5-1 thrashing of Southampton at St James' Park...and Chelsea's John Spencer hits two in the Blues' 3-2 away victory at Leeds.

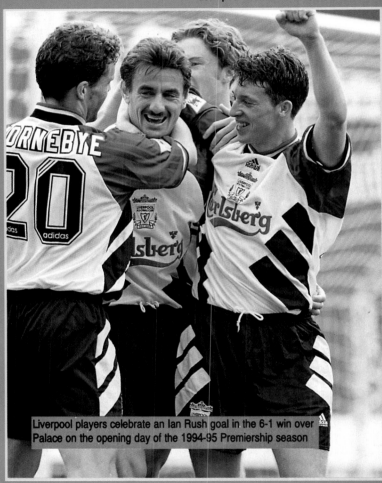

Liverpool players celebrate an Ian Rush goal in the 6-1 win over Palace on the opening day of the 1994-95 Premiership season

SUNDAY 28th
Young Robbie Fowler sets a new Premiership record by completing a devastating hat-trick in 4 minutes 33 seconds as Liverpool overwhelm Arsenal 3-0 at Anfield.

MONDAY 29th
Aston Villa record their first win of the season - a 1-0 victory over midlands rivals Coventry at Highfield Road.

TUESDAY 30th
Leeds get back on track with a 2-1 away win against Crystal Palace. Jurgen

Klinsmann scores twice for Spurs in a 3-1 victory at Ipswich. Forest beat Everton 2-1 at Goodison Park.

WEDNESDAY 31st
Chelsea beat Machester City 3-0 in a downpour. It's the Blues' third win of the

season and marks their best start in 30 years. Eric Cantona marks his return to first team action, after a ban, by scoring in Manchester United's 3-0 home win against Wimbledon. Leicester collect their first Premiership point thanks to a 1-1 draw with QPR. Newcastle win 3-1 at West Ham; Hammers' new signing Don Hutchison scores from the penalty-spot. August ends with Newcastle on top of the table with a 100% record, followed by Manchester United, Nottingham Forest, Liverpool and Chelsea. Everton, Leicester, West Ham and Coventry occupy the four relegation places.

SEPTEMBER -
SATURDAY 10th
The Premiership programme resumes after a week of European Championship and friendly international action. Aston Villa chalk up their first home win of the season, 2-0 against Ipswich. Everton go down 3-0 at Blackburn - Alan Shearer scores twice. Newcastle consolidate their position at the top of the table with a 4-2 home win against Chelsea - Andy Cole scores twice. Forest thrash Sheffield Wednesday 4-1 at the City Ground. Dion Dublin scores on his debut for Coventry in a 2-2 away draw with QPR. Three players are sent off in Wimbledon's 2-1 home win against Leicester.

SUNDAY 11th
Leeds win 2-1 in a classic game with Manchester United at Elland Road. David Wetherall and Brian Deane score for Leeds, Eric Cantona replies for United from the penalty-spot.

MONDAY 12th
Matthew Le Tissier scores twice as Southampton beat Spurs 2-1 at White Hart Lane. Jurgen Klinsmann had opened the scoring for Tottenham in the 6th minute.

SATURDAY 17th
New skipper Dion Dublin scores for Coventry as the Sky Blues beat Leeds 2-1 at Highfield Road. Daniel Amokachi scores on his home debut in Everton's 2-2 draw with QPR. Les Ferdinand scores both Rangers' goals. Julian Joachim scores twice as Leicester chalk up their first Premiership victory - 3-1 against Spurs at Filbert Street. Tony Cottee marks his return to West Ham with the only goal of the game against Aston Villa. Manchester United beat Liverpool 2-0 at Old Trafford. The goals from Andrei Kanchelskis and Brian McClair came in the space of a minute late in the second half.

SUNDAY 18th
Peter Beardsley is Man of the Match as Newcastle beat Arsenal 3-2 at Highbury. Blackburn beat Chelsea 2-1 at Stamford Bridge.

MONDAY 19th
Norwich win the East Anglian derby at Ipswich by a 2-1 margin.

SATURDAY 24th
Alan Shearer scores twice as Blackburn beat Villa 3-1 at Ewood Park. Iain Dowie hits two for Southampton in a brilliant 3-1 away win against Coventry. Dion Dublin replies for the Sky Blues. Ipswich record their first home win in seven months - and they do it in style, beating Manchester United 3-2. Paul Mason hits two of Town's goals. Liverpool crack Newcastle's 100% record with a 1-1 draw at St James' Park. Spurs are thrashed 4-1 at home by Nottingham Forest. The dazzling Dutchman Bryan Roy scores twice for Forest.

SUNDAY 25th
Arsenal beat struggling West Ham 2-0 at Upton Park. Tony Adams and Ian Wright are the scorers.

MONDAY 26th
Sheffield Wednesday and Leeds United share the points in the Yorkshire derby at Hillsborough. Mark Bright scores for Wednesday, Gary McAllister for Leeds.

Coventry new boy Dion Dublin challenges for the ball with QPR's Alan McDonald

Leeds United's David White chases Eric Cantona of Manchester United

17

OCTOBER

SATURDAY 1st

Crystal Palace chalk up their first win of the campaign, a 2-1 away defeat of Arsenal. Steve McManaman hits a hat-trick in Liverpool's 4-1 demolition of Sheffield Wednesday at Anfield. Noel Whelan hits both Leeds United goals in a 2-0 home win over Manchester City. Bottom of the table Everton are beaten 2-0 at Manchester United. Norwich end Blackburn's unbeaten run with a 2-1 victory at Carrow Road.

SUNDAY 2nd

West Ham win 2-1 in the London derby against Chelsea at Stamford Bridge. Forest beat QPR 3-2 at the City Ground. Two players are sent off in the 2-2 draw between Leicester and Coventry at Filbert Street.

SATURDAY 8th

John Spencer scores twice in Chelsea's 4-0 drubbing of Leicester at Stamford Bridge. Manchester City and Nottingham Forest battle for a thrilling 3-3 draw at Maine Road. Niall Quinn scores two for City and Stan Collymore hits two for Forest. Everton's woes increase with a 2-0 defeat at Southampton. Arsenal win 3-1 at Wimbledon.

SUNDAY 9th

Newcastle rescue their unbeaten record with a late equaliser against Blackburn at St James' Park: result 1-1.

MONDAY 10th

Coventry beat Ipswich 2-0 at Highfield Road.

SATURDAY 15th

Ian Wright scores twice in Arsenal's 3-1 home victory over Chelsea. Chris Sutton hits two as Blackburn beat Liverpool 3-2 at Ewood Park. Peter Beardsley hits a late goal as table-toppers Newcastle win 1-0 at Crystal Palace. Everton lose 2-0 at home to Coventry. At Filbert Street, Leicester win by the odd goal in seven against Southampton. Manchester City win 2-1 at QPR, despite being reduced to nine-men for the last 18 minutes of the match.

SUNDAY 16th

Bonto Guentchev misses a penalty as Ipswich's woes increase with a 2-1 home defeat by Sheffield Wednesday.

MONDAY 17th

Stan Collymore hits his ninth goal of the campaign as Nottingham Forest step up their challenge for top spot, with a 3-1 home win against Wimbledon.

SATURDAY 22nd

Forest make it 23 games unbeaten with a 2-0 away victory at Aston Villa. Everton's troubles worsen with a 1-0 defeat at Crystal Palace. Spurs' defence crumbles as Manchester City win 5-2 at Maine Road. Newcastle remain unbeaten thanks to a 2-1 home win against Sheffield Wednesday. Norwich beat QPR 4-2 in a Carrow Road thriller. Julian Dicks returns to Upton Park as West Ham beat Southampton 2-0.

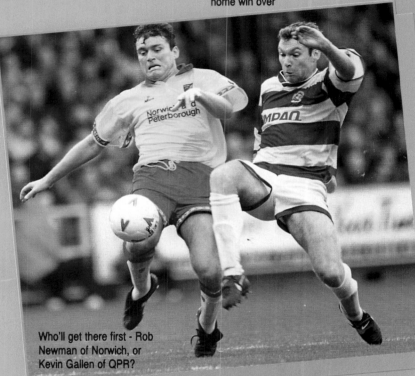

Who'll get there first - Rob Newman of Norwich, or Kevin Gallen of QPR?

SUNDAY 23rd

Ian Wright creates a new Arsenal record, having scored in ten consecutive matches. He hits two in the Gunners' 2-1 home win against Coventry. Manchester United win 4-2 in the battle of the giants against Blackburn at Ewood Park. Andrei Kanchelskis scores twice for United. Denis Wise and Neil Shipperley score late second half goals in Chelsea's 2-0 defeat of Ipswich at Stamford Bridge.

MONDAY 24th

Leeds beat Leicester 2-1 in a hard-fought game at Elland Road.

SATURDAY 29th

Manchester United end Newcastle's unbeaten run with a 2-0 win at Old Trafford, but the Magpies stay top of the table. Forest's unbeaten run also comes to an end with a 2-0 home defeat by Blackburn. Chris Sutton hits both Rovers' goals. Rod Wallace scores twice in Leeds' 3-2 away defeat of Southampton. Robbie Fowler gets two in Liverpool's 3-1 victory over Ipswich at Portman Road. Aston Villa drop into the danger zone after a 2-0 defeat at QPR. Everton secure a point in a 1-1 home draw with Arsenal.

SUNDAY 30th

Struggling Wimbledon chalk up a 1-0 home win over Norwich, thanks to an Efan Ekoku goal.

MONDAY 31st

Liverpool go down 2-1 at QPR who chalk up their second victory in three days.

NOVEMBER

TUESDAY 1st
Bottom-of-the-table Everton secure their first victory of the season with a 1-0 home win over West Ham. Gary Ablett heads the winner in the 54th minute. Ipswich beat Leeds 2-0 at Portman Road. Ossie Ardiles loses his job as manager of Tottenham Hotspur; he is temporarily replaced by Steve Perryman.

WEDNESDAY 2nd
Andy Preece hits two in Crystal Palace's 4-1 demolition of Coventry at Highfield Road. Blackburn move up to second place after a 1-0 away win at Sheffield Wednesday - Alan Shearer gets the goal. A disputed Matthew Le Tissier penalty secures Southampton a 1-1 draw with Norwich at The Dell.

SATURDAY 5th
Manchester City and Southampton provide the Guy Fawkes Day fireworks with a sparkling 3-3 draw at Maine Road. Paul Walsh bangs in two for City; Ronnie Ekelund two for the Saints. Spurs' troubles worsen with a 2-0 damp squib of a defeat at Blackburn. Crystal Palace rocket to their fifth successive victory with a 3-0 win over Ipswich - Newman, Armstrong and Salako are the scorers. West Ham's Don Hutchison is sent off against Leicester, then sent home by manager Harry Redknapp. Hammers win 1-0.

SUNDAY 6th
Manchester United add to Aston Villa's woes with a 2-1 win at Villa Park. Chelsea and Coventry draw 2-2 at Stamford Bridge. Coventry's Dion Dublin proves what a good buy he has been, with yet another goal.

MONDAY 7th
Championship contenders Forest and Newcastle share the points in a 0-0 draw at the City Ground.

TUESDAY 8th
Mike Walker loses his job as manager of Everton, just ten months after leaving Norwich City.

WEDNESDAY 9th
Good news for Spurs...An FA arbitration panel have decided that the north-London club will not have six points deducted from their Premiership total after all. The club has also been reinstated in the FA Cup competition. Dean Saunders scores twice for Villa against Wimbledon at Selhurst Park, but

Dons' debutant Oyvind Leonhardson snatches the winner in a seven-goal thriller. Liverpool beat Chelsea 3-1 at Anfield. Robbie Fowler scores twice for the Reds.

THURSDAY 10th
Manchester United record their biggest ever derby win by thrashing Manchester City 5-0 at Old Trafford. Andrei Kanchelskis hits a hat-trick; the other goals come from Eric Cantona and Mark Hughes. Former Goodison Park favourite Joe Royle is appointed manager at Everton. Ron Atkinson loses his job as manager of Aston Villa.

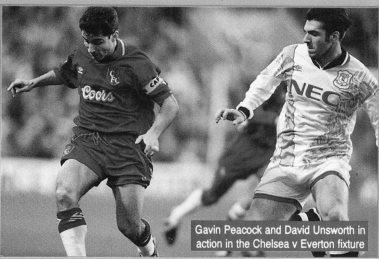

Gavin Peacock and David Unsworth in action in the Chelsea v Everton fixture

FRIDAY 11th
Gerry Francis resigns as manager of QPR.

TUESDAY 15th
Gerry Francis is appointed manager of Tottenham Hotspur. Ray Wilkins becomes manager at QPR

SATURDAY 19th
The Premiership programme resumes after a week off for international action (England have beaten Nigeria 1-0). Manchester United go top of the table after a 3-0 defeat of Crystal Palace. Ray Wilkins celebrates his first match in charge at QPR with a 3-2 home win against Leeds. Meanwhile new Spurs boss Gerry Francis sees his side go down 4-3 at home to Aston Villa. Blackburn chalk up their fifth successive league victory, 3-1 away to Ipswich. Newcastle slip with a 3-2 away defeat at Wimbledon.

SUNDAY 20th
Thanks to a Niall Quinn goal, Manchester City beat Leicester 1-0 at

Filbert Street.

MONDAY 21st
Everton's new manager Joe Royle gets off to a dream start with a 2-0 home victory against Liverpool. Duncan Ferguson and Paul Rideout are the scorers.

TUESDAY 22nd
Brian Little resigns as manager of Leicester City; Allan Evans takes over as caretaker manager.

WEDNESDAY 23rd
Leicester score an impressive 2-1 home victory over Arsenal and lift themselves off the bottom of the table.

FRIDAY 25th
Brian Little becomes manager of Aston Villa. Allan Evans resigns at Leicester and is replaced as 'caretaker managers' by Tony McAndrew and Kevin MacDonald.

SATURDAY 26th
Alan Shearer hits a magnificent hat-trick in Blackburn's 4-0 thrashing of QPR at Ewood Park. Everton's revival continues with a 1-0 win at Chelsea; Paul Rideout is the scorer. Spurs salvage a point in a 1-1 draw with Liverpool at Anfield, the equaliser is an own-goal by ex-Spurs star Neil Ruddock. Andy Cole returns for Newcastle and celebrates with a goal against Ipswich. But the East Anglian side rescue the situation with a last minute equaliser by Claus Thomsen.

SUNDAY 27th
Aston Villa draw their first match under new management; 1-1 at home to Sheffield Wednesday.

19

DECEMBER

SATURDAY 3rd

Teddy Sheringham hits a hat-trick as Spurs put on a brilliant display to beat Newcastle 4-2 at White Hart Lane. Ruel Fox scores both the Magpies' goals. Blackburn chalk up a decisive 3-0 victory away to Wimbledon. Nottingham Forest end a goalless spell by scoring twice against Arsenal at The City Ground; but the Gunners reply with two of their own. Brian Little returns to Filbert Street for the first time as Aston Villa's boss. The points are shared as the two teams draw a tension-filled match 1-1. An Eric Cantona goal secures Manchester United's 1-0 victory at home to Norwich.

SUNDAY 4th

West Ham drop into the relegation zone following a 2-1 defeat by QPR at Loftus Road.

MONDAY 5th

John Lyall resigns as Ipswich Town manager. Ray Goddard is appointed caretaker manager at Portman Road. The Everton revival continues with a fine 3-0 win over Leeds at Goodison Park. The Toffees are now unbeaten in six games.

SATURDAY 10th

Alan Shearer hits two goals as Blackburn retain their place at the top of the table with a 3-2 home win against Southampton. Matt Le Tissier scores both the Saints' goals. Everton continue their unbeaten run with a 0-0 draw at Aston Villa. West Ham fight back from 2-0 down to draw 2-2 with Leeds at Elland Road. Spurs also rally against Sheffield Wednesday at White Hart Lane - the north Londoners go from 1-0 down to a 3-1 victory. Newcastle increase Leicester's worries with a 3-1 win at St James' Park. Paul Scholes scores twice in Manchester United's 3-2 away win at QPR. New boy Ashley Ward hits two goals in Norwich's 3-0 destruction of Chelsea at Carrow Road. Forest hit four past Ipswich at the City Ground - Ipswich reply with a consolation goal.

MONDAY 12th

Arsenal win 2-1 at Manchester City, with goals from Alan Smith and Stefan Schwarz.

WEDNESDAY 14th

Mark McGhee resigns as manager of Reading to take over the Leicester City hot-seat.

FRIDAY 16th

Ipswich have to equalise twice to salvage a 2-2 draw with Wimbledon at Portman Road.

SATURDAY 17th

An exciting final four minutes at Highbury, gives Leeds a 3-1 victory against Arsenal. Everton set a new club record of seven successive League games without defeat after a 0-0 draw with Spurs at Goodison Park. Tony Cottee strikes a magnificent hat-trick to give West Ham a 3-0 home win over Manchester City. With a 2-1 scoreline Forest inflict Manchester United's first home defeat of the season. Coventry keeper Steve Ogrisovic saves an Andy Cole penalty at Highfield Road to preserve a 0-0 scoreline against Newcastle.

SUNDAY 18th

Chelsea hold Liverpool to a 0-0 draw at Anfield.

MONDAY 19th

A magnificent 25-yard goal by Matt Le Tissier gives Southampton a last-minute winner against Aston Villa at The Dell: result 2-1.

MONDAY 26th

Plenty of Boxing Day action...Manchester United win 3-2 against Chelsea at Stamford Bridge, after the Blues had pulled back a two-goal deficit. Sheffield Wednesday bring Everton down to earth with a 4-1 thrashing at Goodison Park. Blackburn press their claim on the title with a 3-1 away win against Manchester City. Liverpool beat ten-man Leicester 2-1 at Filbert Street. Spurs become the first victors of the season at Norwich, with a 2-0 win. Wimbledon chalk up a 3-2 win in an entertaining game against Southampton at The Dell; Dean Holdsworth scores twice for the Dons.

WEDNESDAY 28th

Former Colchester United boss George Burley is appointed manager of Ipswich, but gets off to a troubled start with a 2-0 home defeat by Arsenal. Aston Villa sting Chelsea 3-0 at Villa Park. Leicester hold Manchester United to a 1-1 draw at Old Trafford. Guy Whittingham and Mark Bright both score twice for Sheffield Wednesday in a 5-1 drubbing of Coventry at Hillsborough.

SATURDAY 31st

1994 closes with some more brilliant Premiership action...Paul Rideout scores twice as Everton beat Ipswich 4-1 at Goodison Park. Crystal Palace lose 1-0 at home to high flying Blackburn. Spurs thrash coventry 4-0 at Highfield Road. After eleven attempts QPR finally beat Arsenal at Highbury, by a 3-1 scoreline. West Ham score a decisive 3-1 home win over Forest. Uwe Rosler hits both Manchester City's goals in their 2-2 draw with Aston Villa at Maine Road. Manchester United twice come from behind to draw 2-2 at Southampton. Leeds go down 2-0 to Liverpool at Elland Road.

West Ham's Tony Cottee gets in a shot against QPR

JANUARY

MONDAY 2nd
It's a happy start to the New Year for Liverpool who win 4-0 at Norwich...Ipswich who win 4-1 at Portman Road against fellow strugglers Leicester...and Blackburn who win 4-2 at home to West Ham, a game which includes an Alan Shearer hat-trick. Spurs beat north-London neighbours Arsenal 1-0 at White Hart Lane.

TUESDAY 3rd
Manchester United increase the pressure at the top end of the table with a 2-0 home win over Coventry.

WEDNESDAY 11th
The football world reels at the news of Andy Cole's £7 million move from Newcastle to Manchester United. £1 million-rated Keith Gillespie travels from Old Trafford to St James' Park as part of the deal.

SATURDAY 14th
Normal service resumes in the Premiership after the previous weekend's FA Cup Third Round action...Aston Villa achieve only their third home victory of the campaign, beating QPR 2-1.
Blackburn chalk-up a decisive 3-0 home victory over Forest. After nine Premiership games Crystal Palace finally find the net and end up beating Leicester 2-0 at Selhurst Park. Ipswich ease their troubles with a 1-0 defeat of Liverpool at Anfield. Spurs beat West Ham 2-1 at Upton Park. Wimbledon beat Norwich 2-1 at Carrow Road.

SUNDAY 15th
Newcastle and Manchester United draw 1-1 at St James' Park. Andy Cole does not play in the match.

SATURDAY 21st
John Hartson, Arsenal's new £2.5 million striker from Luton, scores his first goal for the Gunners in a 1-0 away win at Coventry. Duncan Ferguson scores twice for Everton in a 3-1 relegation zone victory over Crystal Palace. Chelsea's Craig Burley scores a last-minute equaliser against Ipswich who are managed by his uncle, George: result 2-2. Five Premiership matches are postponed because of bad weather.

SUNDAY 22nd
In the top of the table clash Manchester United beat Blackburn 1-0, thanks to a brilliant header by Eric Cantona.

MONDAY 23rd
West Ham's Alvin Martin is controversially sent-off early in the match against Sheffield Wednesday at Upton Park. His team-mate Tim Breacker also gets his marching orders. Wednesday win 2-0.

TUESDAY 24th
Phil Massinga hits two goals as Leeds thrash QPR 4-0 at Elland Road. The Merseyside derby at Goodison Park ends in a 0-0 stalemate.

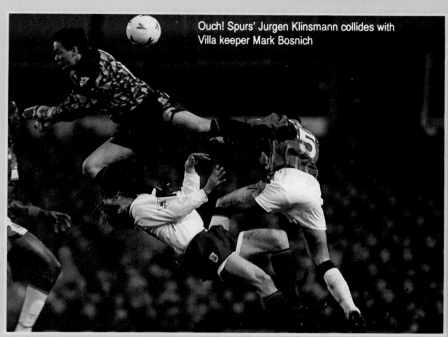
Ouch! Spurs' Jurgen Klinsmann collides with Villa keeper Mark Bosnich

WEDNESDAY 25th
The world is stunned by the infamous 'Eric Cantona incident' which occurs in Manchester United's 1-1 draw with Crystal Palace at Selhurst Park. Spurs' Jurgen Klinsmann is carried off after a collision with Villa keeper Mark Bosnich, as Villa win 1-0 at home. Stan Collymore hits both goals in Forest's away win against Chelsea. Mark Robins scores on his debut for Leicester, in a 1-0 away win at Manchester City.

SATURDAY 28th
In the only Premiership match of the day, Blackburn beat Ipswich 4-1 at Ewood Park. Alan Shearer scores a hit trick. Rovers end the month at the top of the table, four points ahead of Manchester United and with a game in hand.

FEBRUARY

WEDNESDAY 1st
Premiership leaders Blackburn draw 1-1 with Leeds at Ewood Park. Everton have two players sent-off in a 2-0 defeat at Newcastle.

SATURDAY 4th
Andy Cole scores his first goal for Manchester United in a 1-0 home win against Villa. Les Ferdinand scores twice in QPR's 3-0 home win over injury-hit Newcastle. Everton improve their survival chances with a 2-1 home victory over Norwich. Sheffield Wednesday beat Arsenal 3-1 at Hillsborough - it's the Owls' first victory against the Gunners since 1993. Ipswich's troubles worsen with a 2-0 home defeat by Crystal Palace.

SUNDAY 5th
Spurs beat table toppers Blackburn 3-1 in a stylish game at White Hart Lane.

SATURDAY 11th
Aston Villa chalk-up a magnificent 7-1 home win against Wimbledon - a Premiership record and Villa's biggest win in 33 years. Tommy Johnson hits a hat-trick and Dean Saunders scores twice in the match. In his first game since his personal problems were made public, Paul Merson scores for Arsenal in a 1-1 draw with Leicester at Highbury. In the Manchester derby at Maine Road, United beat City 3-0.

SUNDAY 12th
Blackburn resume their title challenge with a 3-1 home victory over Sheffield Wednesday.

MONDAY 13th
Tony Cottee scores twice for West Ham in a 2-2 draw with his old club Everton at Upton Park.

TUESDAY 14th
Coventry manager Phil Neal resigns.

WEDNESDAY 15th
Ron Atkinson is appointed manager of Coventry City.

SATURDAY 18th
Coventry's new boss Ron Atkinson sees his side win 2-0 at home against West Ham. Dean Saunders hits two goals as Villa beat Sheffield Wednesday 2-1 at Hillsborough.

TUESDAY 21st
Arsenal manager George Graham is

sacked; he is replaced by Stewart Houston as caretaker manager. The Gunners then beat Forest 1-0 at Highbury.

WEDNESDAY 22nd
A brilliant Leicester comeback earns them a 4-4 draw at Aston Villa. Blackburn stay on target with a 2-1 home win against Wimbledon. Manchester United stay in touch with a 2-0 away defeat of Norwich. Tony Yeboah scores on his full debut for Leeds, in a 1-0 home victory over Everton.

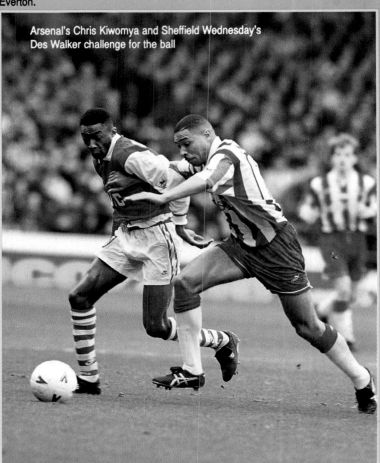

Arsenal's Chris Kiwomya and Sheffield Wednesday's Des Walker challenge for the ball

SATURDAY 25th
Efan Ekoku scores both Wimbledon's goals in a 2-1 win at Tottenham. Peter Beardsley scores twice in Newcastle's 3-1 home win over Villa. Sean Flynn hits two goals for Coventry at Highfield Road in a 4-2 win over relegation-threatened Leicester. Chris Kiwomya also gets two for Arsenal who win 3-0 at Crystal Palace. Everton beat Manchester United 1-0 at Goodison Park, while Norwich hold Blackburn 0-0 at Carrow Road.

SUNDAY 26th
A late strike by Simon Barker salvages a point for QPR in a 1-1 draw with Nottingham Forest at Loftus Road.

TUESDAY 28th
Ipswich drop more precious points in a 2-0 home defeat by Newcastle.

MARCH

SATURDAY 4th
Manchester United smash Aston Villa's briefly-held Premiership 'biggest victory' record, by beating Ipswich 9-0 at Old Trafford. Andy Cole hits five of United's goals, and Mark Hughes gets two (the others come from Roy Keane and Paul Ince). Liverpool beat Newcastle 2-0 at Anfield. Blackburn press on with a 1-0 away win at Villa. Leicester draw 2-2 at home to Everton, thanks to a late Iwan Roberts strike.

SUNDAY 5th
West Ham beat Arsenal 1-0 at Highbury. It's the Gunners' first defeat under Stewart Houston's managership. Chelsea and Crystal Palace draw 0-0 at Stamford Bridge.

MONDAY 6th
Aston Villa and Coventry draw 0-0 in the midlands derby at Villa Park.

TUESDAY 7th
A late goal by Steve Bruce gives Manchester United a 1-0 away victory over Wimbledon.

WEDNESDAY 8th
Alan Shearer scores twice in Blackburn's 3-1 home win against Arsenal. Chelsea win 2-1 at Manchester City; Mark Stein scores both the Blues' goals. Spurs beat Ipswich 3-0 at White Hart Lane.

SATURDAY 11th
Leeds beat Chelsea 3-0 at Stamford Bridge; Tony Yeboah scores two of United's goals. Coventry hold Blackburn 1-1 at Highfield Road. Leicester's woes increase with a 4-2 home defeat by Forest. Down to ten men, Norwich almost beat West Ham at Upton Park, but two late goals from Tony Cottee saves the day for the Hammers: result 2-2.

TUESDAY 14th
A brilliant Peter Ndlovu hat-trick earns Coventry a famous 3-2 victory over Liverpool at Anfield. Crystal Palace go down 1-0 at Sheffield Wednesday.

WEDNESDAY 15th
Leeds beat injury-hit Leicester 3-1 at Filbert Street. Manchester United and Spurs draw 0-0 at Old Trafford. It's the first time United have not scored at home all season.

SATURDAY 18th
West Ham win 2-0 in the clash of the 'claret and blues' at Villa Park. Blackburn beat Chelsea 2-1 at Ewood Park. Manchester City stage a fine fight back to take all the points with a 3-2 victory over Sheffield Wednesday at Maine road. Bryan Roy scores twice in Forest's 3-0 win against Southampton at the City Ground. Wimbledon beat their 'landlords' Palace 2-0 at Selhurst Park.

SUNDAY 19th
Liverpool dent Manchester United's title hopes with a 2-0 victory at Anfield. Newcastle record their first league 'double' over Arsenal in 28 years. A Peter Beardsley goal gives the Magpies a 1-0 victory.

MONDAY 20th
Norwich win the East Anglian derby 3-0 at Carrow Road.

TUESDAY 21st
Wimbledon beat Manchester City 2-0 at Selhurst Park.

WEDNESDAY 22nd
Manchester United get back on track with a 3-0 defeat of Arsenal at Old Trafford. QPR win 2-0 in the West London derby against Chelsea. Bryan Roy scores twice in Forest's 3-0 home win against Leeds. Southampton stage a great comeback to beat Newcastle 3-1 at the Dell.

Newcastle ace Peter Beardsley scored the winner against Arsenal

APRIL

SATURDAY 1st
The Premiership programme resumes following international action (England drew 0-0 with Uruguay at Wembley). Nottingham Forest thrash Sheffield Wednesday 7-1 at Hillsborough - Stan Collymore and Bryan Roy score two goals each. John Hartson scores a hat-trick as Arsenal thrash Norwich 5-1 at Highbury. Wimbledon win a seven-goal thriller 4-3 against Leicester at Filbert Street. Blackburn beat Everton 2-1 at Goodison Park. Crystal Palace ease their relegation worries with a 2-1 home victory against Manchester City.

SUNDAY 2nd
Southampton win a seven-goal thriller against Spurs, 4-3 at the Dell. Matt Le Tissier scores twice for the Saints, Teddy Sheringham scores twice for Tottenham. Leeds hold Manchester United 0-0 at Old Trafford.

TUESDAY 4th
Blackburn edge a little closer to the title with a 1-0 away win at QPR.

SATURDAY 8th
Newcastle increase Norwich's woes with a 3-0 win at St James' Park. Sheffield Wednesday do the same for Leicester with a 1-0 win at Hillsborough. QPR ensure their Premiership safety with a 3-1 win over Arsenal at Loftus Road.

SUNDAY 9th
Leeds beat Liverpool 1-0 away, with a Brian Deane goal. It's the first time Leeds have beaten the Reds at Anfield since 1971-72!

MONDAY 10th
A second half fightback earns Wimbledon a 1-1 draw with Chelsea at Stamford Bridge.

TUESDAY 11th
QPR beat Ipswich 1-0 at Portman Road. Ipswich have not scored in seven successive defeats.

WEDNESDAY 12th
Three away wins as - Southampton beat Chelsea 2-0 at Stamford Bridge, Liverpool beat Arsenal 1-0 at Highbury and Forest beat Norwich 1-0 at Carrow Road.

THURSDAY 13th
West Ham improve their survival chances by hammering Wimbledon 3-0 at Upton Park.

FRIDAY 14th
Manchester City outplay Liverpool for a 2-1 victory at Maine Road. Daniel Amokachi scores twice for Everton to ensure an important 2-0 home win against Newcastle. Jurgen Klinsmann's late goal secures a point for Spurs in a 1-1 draw with Crystal Palace at Selhurst Park.

SATURDAY 15th
Ian Wright scores twice in Arsenal's 4-1 home victory over luckless Ipswich.

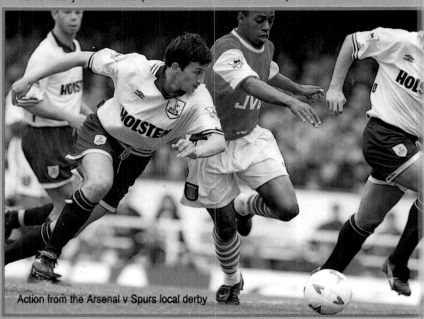
Action from the Arsenal v Spurs local derby

Andy Cole hits two past Leicester in Manchester United's 4-0 win at Filbert Street. Blackburn draw 1-1 at Leeds. Coventry ensure their Premiership survival with a 2-0 home win over Sheffield Wednesday. Chelsea improve their safety prospects with a 1-0 home win over Villa. Southampton beat QPR 2-1 at the Dell.

MONDAY 17th
Blackburn's title challenge stumbles with a 3-2 home defeat by Manchester City. City came from behind twice to win a brilliant game. Manchester United draw 0-0 with Chelsea at Old Trafford. Arsenal add to Aston Villa's worries with a 4-0 win at Villa Park - John Hartson and Ian Wright score two goals each. Leeds beat Newcastle 2-1 at St James' Park, to mark the Magpies' first home defeat in over 15 months. Crystal Palace grab three vital points with a 1-0 victory at QPR. Norwich lose 1-0 at Tottenham. A last minute equaliser by Jeroen Boere at Ipswich earns West Ham a 1-1 draw.

THURSDAY 20th
Blackburn get back on track with a 2-1 home win against Crystal Palace.

SATURDAY 29th
In the North London derby at Highbury Arsenal and Spurs share the points in a 1-1 draw. In the West London derby at Stamford Bridge, Chelsea beat QPR 1-0. Crystal Palace lose 2-1 at home to Forest. Aston Villa go down 1-0 at Leeds. In the battle of the bottom clubs Leicester beat Ipswich 2-0 at Filbert Street. Substitute goalkeeper John Burridge makes his debut for Manchester City at the age of 43, and he keeps a clean sheet - in a 0-0 draw with Newcastle at Maine Road. Norwich lose 2-1 at home to Liverpool.

SUNDAY 30th
The championship race takes an unexpected turn as West Ham beat leaders Blackburn 2-0 at Upton Park.

MAY

MONDAY 1st
Andy Cole scores twice as Manchester United close the gap at the top with a 3-2 win at Coventry.

TUESDAY 2nd
Wimbledon and Liverpool draw 0-0 at Selhurst Park.

WEDNESDAY 3rd
Everton and Chelsea are involved in a thrilling 3-3 draw at Goodison Park. At St James' Park Newcastle and Spurs also draw 3-3. Aston Villa and Manchester City draw 1-1 at Villa Park. West Ham and QPR share the points in a 0-0 draw at Upton Park. Matt Le Tissier scores twice in Southampton's 3-1 home victory over Crystal Palace.

THURSDAY 4th
European Cup-Winners' Cup finalists Arsenal draw 0-0 with Wimbledon at Highbury.

SATURDAY 6th
Norwich City's relegation is confirmed after a 2-1 defeat by Leeds at Elland Road. Crystal Palace grab three valuable points with a 1-0 home win against West Ham. Dwight Yorke scores both of Aston Villa's goals in their 2-0 home win over Liverpool. Nottingham Forest secure third place and a 1995-96 UEFA Cup berth, following a 1-0 home win against Manchester City. Meanwhile, a 2-1 defeat at QPR ends Spurs UEFA Cup hopes. Bottom placed Ipswich beat Coventry 2-0.

SUNDAY 7th
Manchester United's championship challenge is still very much alive, thanks to a 1-0 victory over Sheffield Wednesday at Old Trafford.

MONDAY 8th
Blackburn increase the pressure at the top, with a 1-0 home win against Newcastle.

TUESDAY 9th
Norwich City manager John Deehan resigns; Gary Megson takes over as caretaker manager. Everton's relegation worries are over, following a 1-0 win at Ipswich. Tony Yeboah scores twice in Leeds' brilliant 3-1 win at Crystal Palace. Coventry are safe after a superb 3-1 win at Tottenham; Peter Ndlovu scores twice for the Sky Blues.

WEDNESDAY 10th
A Denis Irwin penalty conversion earns Manchester United a 2-1 victory at Southampton. Don Hutchison scores twice for West Ham in a 3-0 win against Liverpool at Upton Park.

'Let's get on with it!' says Manchester United scorer Brian McClair, as time runs out against West Ham

SATURDAY 13th
Wimbledon and Forest round off their season with a 2-2 draw at Selhurst Park.

SUNDAY 14th
The last day of the 1994-95 Carling Premiership season sees Crystal Palace fill the last relegation spot. Despite a valiant fightback after being three goals down to Newcastle at half-time, Palace still lost 3-2. Aston Villa's Premiership survival is secured with a 1-1 draw at relegated Norwich. Sheffield Wednesday leap to mid-table respectability by beating Ipswich 4-1. Relegated Leicester claw back a two-goal deficit at Southampton to achieve a 2-2 draw. Les Ferdinand scores twice for QPR in a 3-2 win against Manchester City at Maine Road. At the top of the table Manchester United's chance to make it three titles in a row is spoiled by West Ham who hold them to a 1-1 draw at Upton Park. And, despite losing 2-1 at Liverpool, Blackburn Rovers are confirmed champions of the Carling Premiership for 1994-95.

MONDAY 29th
The final place in the Premiership for 1995-96 is settled when Bolton Wanderers beat Reading 4-3 in a thrilling First Division Play-Off Final at Wembley.

The Blackburn bench react to the news that they are the new Carling Premiership champs

BLACKBURN ROVERS THE CHAMPIONS

The title race had gone right down to the wire, but at the end of it all Blackburn Rovers knew they were the Carling Premiership champions of 1994-95...and boy did they celebrate!

Blackburn fans salute their team...and Chris Sutton returns the compliment

Just champion! Blackburn are overjoyed at winning the FA Carling Premiership title

It was a job well done by Rovers' manager Kenny Dalglish

PREMIERSHIP
FACTS
AND
FIGURES
1994-95

BIGGEST WINS
Home – Manchester United 9, Ipswich Town 0
Away – Sheffield Wednesday 1, Nott'm Forest 7

MOST GOALS IN A GAME
9 – Manchester United 9, Ipswich Town 0
8 – Sheffield Wednesday 1, Nott'm Forest 7
– Aston Villa 7, Wimbledon 1
– Aston Villa 4, Leicester City 4

MOST GOALS SCORED

Blackburn Rovers	80
Manchester United	77
Nottingham Forest	72
Newcastle United	67
Tottenham Hotspur	66
Liverpool	65

LEAST GOALS SCORED

Crystal Palace	34
Ipswich Town	36
Norwich City	37
West Ham United	44
Everton	44
Coventry City	44

ATTENDANCES

Total attendance	11,213,168
Highest	43,868 Manchester United v Sheffield Wed
Lowest	5,268 Wimbledon v Manchester City
Highest average attendance	43,682 Manchester United
Lowest average attendance	10,230 Wimbledon

	P	W	D	L	F	A	GD	Pts
1. BLACKBURN ROVERS	42	27	8	7	80	39	+41	89

A brilliant season for Kenny Dalglish's team and an exciting race to the title. Rovers were also Premiership top scorers as they collected their first title since 1914.

	P	W	D	L	F	A	GD	Pts
2. MANCHESTER UNITED	42	26	10	6	77	28	+49	88

United almost made it three in a row, but just couldn't get the better of West Ham on the last day of the season. Also losing FA Cup finalists against Everton.

	P	W	D	L	F	A	GD	Pts
3. NOTTINGHAM FOREST	42	22	11	9	72	43	+29	77

A terrific return to the top flight for Frank Clark's team who can now look forward to a European adventure in the UEFA Cup.

	P	W	D	L	F	A	GD	Pts
4. LIVERPOOL	42	21	11	10	65	37	+28	74

Fourth place was a great improvement on 1993–94 for the Anfield Reds. Also winners of the Coca-Cola Cup against Bolton.

	P	W	D	L	F	A	GD	Pts
5. LEEDS UNITED	42	20	13	9	59	38	+21	73

A late surge by Howard Wilkinson's highly efficient team earned them a well-deserved UEFA Cup berth.

	P	W	D	L	F	A	GD	Pts
6. NEWCASTLE UNITED	42	20	12	10	67	47	+20	72

Kevin Keegan's Magpies began the season really well, but they faded somewhat in the latter stages. Just missed out on a UEFA Cup place.

	P	W	D	L	F	A	GD	Pts
7. TOTTENHAM HOTSPUR	42	16	14	12	66	58	+8	62

Spurs had a better season than expected – especially as they began with the disadvantage of docked points, which were later restored. Striker Jurgen Klinsmann was one of the season's great entertainers.

	P	W	D	L	F	A	GD	Pts
8. QUEENS PARK RANGERS	42	17	9	16	61	59	+2	60

After Gerry Francis' departure to Spurs, Ray Wilkins returned to Loftus Road as team boss and steered Rangers to a two-place improvement on 1993–94.

	P	W	D	L	F	A	GD	Pts
9. WIMBLEDON	42	15	11	16	48	65	−17	56

Joe Kinnear's 'not so crazy gang' continued to compete well with the Premiership's bigger clubs and are still among the most difficult sides to beat.

	P	W	D	L	F	A	GD	Pts
10. SOUTHAMPTON	42	12	18	12	61	63	−2	54

The Saints were the draw specialists of 1994–95. They also created some spectacular goals – thanks largely to the brilliance of Matt Le Tissier.

	P	W	D	L	F	A	GD	Pts
11. CHELSEA	42	13	15	14	50	55	−5	54

A late return to form steered the Blues out of the danger zone. Also enjoyed a fine run to the semi-finals of the European Cup-Winners Cup.

	P	W	D	L	F	A	GD	Pts
12. ARSENAL	42	13	12	17	52	49	+3	51

The Gunners survived internal problems to finish in mid-table. Also reached the final of the European Cup-Winners Cup – and almost retained the trophy.

	P	W	D	L	F	A	GD	Pts
13. SHEFFIELD WEDNESDAY	42	13	12	17	49	57	−8	51

A disappointing campaign for Trevor Francis' Owls who were involved in the relegation battle right up to the last day of the season.

	P	W	D	L	F	A	GD	Pts
14. WEST HAM UNITED	42	13	11	18	44	48	−4	50

The Hammers played their part in the last day drama by holding Manchester United to a 1–1 draw, thereby denying them the title.

	P	W	D	L	F	A	GD	Pts
15. EVERTON	42	11	17	14	44	51	−7	50

Joe Royle's return to Goodison Park as manager did the trick as Everton once again battled to keep out of the drop zone – and they won the FA Cup!

	P	W	D	L	F	A	GD	Pts
16. COVENTRY CITY	42	12	14	16	44	62	−18	50

Despite flirting with danger in the closing weeks of the season, the Sky Blues ensured themselves of a 29th campaign in the top flight.

	P	W	D	L	F	A	GD	Pts
17. MANCHESTER CITY	42	12	13	17	53	64	−11	49

While the red half of Manchester was challenging for the title, the blue half once again struggled at the wrong end of the table.

	P	W	D	L	F	A	GD	Pts
18. ASTON VILLA	42	11	15	16	51	56	−5	48

Villa live to fight again in the Premiership. Their survival was saved on the last day thanks to a 1–1 draw with doomed Norwich at Carrow Road.

RELEGATED

	P	W	D	L	F	A	GD	Pts
19. CRYSTAL PALACE	42	11	12	19	34	49	−15	45

Despite a magnificent fight back in the last game of the season at Newcastle, Palace lost 3–2 and became the last club to make the drop.

	P	W	D	L	F	A	GD	Pts
20. NORWICH CITY	42	10	13	19	37	54	−7	43

A drastic loss of form in the second half of the season sealed the Canaries fate and they could not avoid the drop.

	P	W	D	L	F	A	GD	Pts
21. LEICESTER CITY	42	6	11	25	45	80	−35	29

Leicester struggled throughout their first-ever Premiership season and always looked candidates for the drop.

	P	W	D	L	F	A	GD	Pts
22. IPSWICH TOWN	42	7	6	29	36	93	−57	27

The worst defensive record in the Premiership spelled total disaster for Ipswich who return to the First Division after three seasons in the top flight.

F.A. CARLING PREMIERSHIP

TOP 10

PENALTY KING
ALAN SHEARER
Blackburn Rovers 10

GOALSCORERS 1994-95

Robbie Fowler – 25 goals

Alan Shearer – 34 goals

THE TOP TEN	
1..ALAN SHEARER Blackburn Rovers	34
2..ROBBIE FOWLER Liverpool	25
3..LES FERDINAND QPR.	24
4..STAN COLLYMORE Nottingham Forest	22
5..ANDY COLE Manchester United	21*
6=.JURGEN KLINSMANN Spurs	20
6=.MATTHEW LE TISSIER Southampton	20
8..IAN WRIGHT Arsenal	18
9=.DEAN SAUNDERS Aston Villa	15
9=.CHRIS SUTTON Blackburn Rovers	15
9=.UWE ROSLER Manchester City	15
* total includes goals for Newcastle United	

The Premiership's leading sharp-shooter of 1994–95 was Blackburn's Alan Shearer who contributed an amazing 34 goals to Rovers' championship-winning campaign. Alan was also the penalty-king with ten successful strikes from the spot.

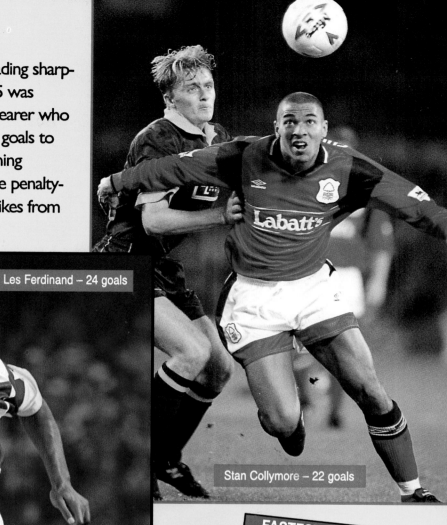

Les Ferdinand – 24 goals

Stan Collymore – 22 goals

FASTEST GOAL
CHRIS SUTTON
Blackburn Rovers v Everton 13 secs

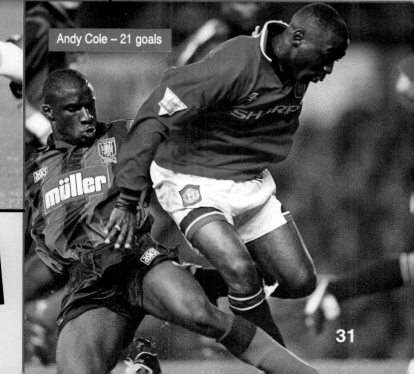

Andy Cole – 21 goals

MOST GOALS IN A GAME –
ANDY COLE
Manchester United 5

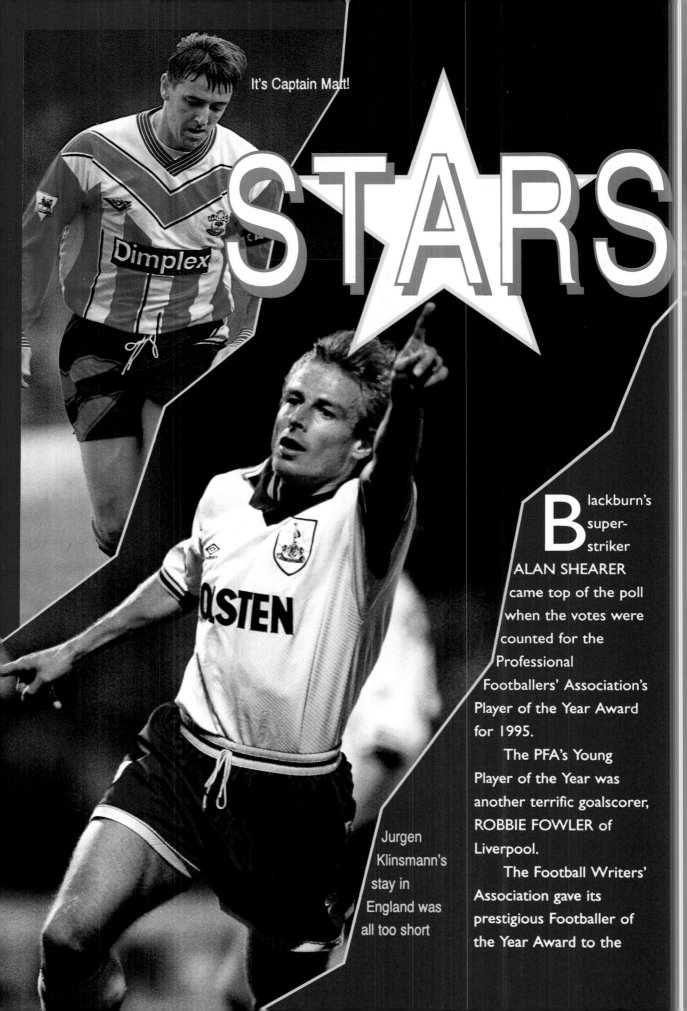

It's Captain Matt!

STARS

Jurgen Klinsmann's stay in England was all too short

Blackburn's super-striker ALAN SHEARER came top of the poll when the votes were counted for the Professional Footballers' Association's Player of the Year Award for 1995.

The PFA's Young Player of the Year was another terrific goalscorer, ROBBIE FOWLER of Liverpool.

The Football Writers' Association gave its prestigious Footballer of the Year Award to the

OF THE ★ SEASON

great entertainer JURGEN KLINSMANN who had such a fine season with Spurs. Another foreign star who made quite an impact was the creative midfielder BRYAN ROY at Nottingham Forest.

Other outstanding Premiership performers in 1994–95 included goalkeeper TIM FLOWERS whose sheer consistency was a major factor in Blackburn's championship success, as was that of COLIN HENDRY, CHRIS SUTTON, GRAEME LE SAUX and skipper TIM SHERWOOD.

Southampton's MATTHEW LE TISSIER provided some great entertainment and some

Blackburn's consistent keeper, Tim Flowers

great goals. PAUL INCE was a driving force behind Manchester United's championship challenge and GARY PALLISTER provided stirling service in United's defence.

Young players NICK BARMBY of Spurs, KEVIN GALLEN of QPR and STEVE McMANAMAN of Liverpool all enjoyed a great season.

The Dutch master, Bryan Roy

Gary Pallister
– the heart of
Manchester
United's
defence

QPR's Kevin gets goals by the Gallen!

Spurs' young hot-shot Nick Barmby

COMING UP

While Blackburn Rovers and Manchester United battled it out for Premiership supremacy, things were every bit as tense at the wrong end of the table – and the unlucky clubs who could not escape the drop were Ipswich Town, Leicester City, Norwich City and Crystal Palace.

The streamlining of the Carling Premiership meant that just two clubs would be promoted from the First Division.

The first promotion place was secured by First Division champions Middlesbrough, led by Bryan Robson in his first season as a manager. This meant that Boro's brand new Riverside Stadium would witness Premiership action in its inaugural season.

The second promotion place was decided by the First Division Play-Offs. In the semi-finals first legs Wolves beat Bolton 2–1 at Molineux, while Reading outfoxed Tranmere at Prenton Park to win 3–1.

In the second legs Bolton's John McGinlay scored both goals in the 2–0 defeat of Wolves,

while Reading held Tranmere to a 0–0 draw.

The Play-Off final at Wembley on 29 May saw Bolton stage a brilliant comeback to beat Reading 4-3 after extra time. It was one of the most thrilling Play-Off matches yet seen.

Reading began in inspired form to go two-up within 12 minutes. Their first goal came from a magnificent solo effort by Lee Nogan who twisted and turned his way through the Bolton defence before firing

home. The second was snatched by Adrian Williams when Bolton were caught napping after a quickly-taken free-kick.

Shortly before half time Reading's Stuart Lovell had the chance to put the game beyond Bolton's reach, with a penalty. But his kick was brilliantly saved by Keith Branagan. Minutes later the unfortunate Lovell missed another golden opportunity.

Bolton began the second half full of fire and determination, but Reading kept them at bay until the 75th minute when Owen Coyle headed them back into the game.

Wanderers' substitute Fabian De Freitas skied the ball over the crossbar in the 80th minute, but he made up for his miss six minutes later by shaking off a Reading challenge and scoring the all-important equaliser to take the match into extra time.

Bolton now looked the stronger of the two teams, and just before the extra time interval Mixu Paatelainen put them ahead for the first time in the match, after a terrific run by Jason McAteer had created the chance.

Supersub De Freitas then struck his second goal of the game, after his initial shot rebounded of the post. Bolton were 4-2 ahead and cruising towards promotion.

But there was still more drama to come. In the last-minute of extra time, Reading's player-manager Jimmy Quinn thundered the ball into the top of the Bolton net. But Reading's revival came too late and time ran out on them.

Bolton Wanderers were in the Carling Premiership.

FIRST DIVISION PLAY-OFF RESULTS
Semi-Final first-leg
Wolves 2, Bolton Wanderers 1
Tranmere Rovers 1, Reading 3
Semi-final second-leg
Bolton Wanderers 2, Wolves 0 (aet)
Reading 0, Tranmere Rovers 0
Final
BOLTON WANDERERS 4, READING 3 (aet) (Half time 0-2)

GOING DOWN

Joy for Middlesbrough – their 1994–95 First Division championship will bring Premiership football to the brand new stadium down by the Riverside

MANCHESTER UNITED

Sir Matt Busby Way, *Old Trafford*, Manchester, M16 ORA. Telephone: 0161-872 1661. Ticket Information: 0161-872 0199. Fax: 0161-876 5502.
Chairman/Chief Executive: C.M. Edwards
Manager: Alex Ferguson
Youth Development Officer: P. McGuiness
Sponsors: Sharp Electronics
Nickname: 'The Red Devils'
Colours: Red shirts, white shorts, black socks
2nd strip: All black
Pitch size: 114 x 76 yards
Ground Capacity: 44,487

HONOURS

League Champions: 1907–08, 1910–11, 1951–52, 1955–56, 1956–57, 1964–65, 1966–67, 1992–93, 1993–94 (9)
FA Cup Winners: 1909, 1948, 1963, 1977, 1983, 1985, 1990, 1994 (8)
League Cup Winners: 1992 (1)
Charity Shield Winners: 1908, 1911, 1952, 1956, 1957, 1965 – shared, 1967 – shared, 1977 – shared, 1983, 1993 (10)
European Cup Winners: 1968 (1)
European Cup-Winners' Cup Winners: 1991 (1)
European Super Cup Winners: 1991 (1)

PREMIERSHIP PERFORMANCE 1994–95

P	W	D	L	F	A	GD	Pts	Pos
42	26	10	6	77	28	+49	88	2nd

Leading Scorer: Andrei Kanchelskis (14)
Highest Attendance: 43,868

Cellnet Riverside Stadium, Middlehaven, Middlesbrough, Cleveland, TS3 6RS. Telephone: 01642 819659. Ticket office: 01642 815996. Fax: 01642 829244
Chairman: S .Gibson
Manager: Bryan Robson
Youth Development Officer: Ron Bone
Sponsors: Cellnet
Nickname: 'The Boro'
Colours: Red shirts, white shorts, red socks
2nd strip: Blue and black striped shirts, blue shorts, blue/black socks
Pitch size: 115 x 75 yards
Ground Capacity: 30,000

FIRST DIVISION PERFORMANCE 1994–95

P	W	D	L	F	A	GD	Pts	Pos
46	23	13	10	67	40	+27	82	1st

Leading Scorer: John Hendrie (15)
Highest Attendance: 23,903

MIDDLESBROUGH

NEWCASTLE UNITED

St James' Park, Newcastle-upon-Tyne, NE1 4ST. Telephone: 0191-232-8361. Fax: 0191-232 9875
Chairman: Sir John Hall
Manager: Kevin Keegan
Youth Development Officer: C. McMenemy
Sponsors: Newcastle Breweries
Nickname: 'The Magpies'
Colours: Black & white striped shirts, black shorts, black socks/white trim
2nd strip: Red/blue hooped shirts, white shorts, red/blue socks
Pitch size: 114 x 74 yards
Ground Capacity: 32,372

HONOURS
League Champions: 1904–05, 1906–07, 1908–09, 1926–27 (4)
FA Cup Winners: 1910, 1924, 1932, 1951, 1952, 1955 (6)
Charity Shield Winners: 1909 (1)
UEFA Cup Winners: 1969 (1)

PREMIERSHIP PERFORMANCE 1994–95

P	W	D	L	F	A	GD	Pts	Pos
42	20	12	10	67	47	+20	72	6th

Leading Scorer: Peter Beardsley (13)
Highest Attendance: 35,626

City Ground, Nottingham NG2 5FJ. Telephone: 01602 526000. Fax: 01602 526003.
Chairman: F. Reacher
Manager: Frank Clark
Youth Development Officer: M. Raynor
Sponsors: Labatt's
Nickname: 'Forest'
Colours: Red shirts, white shorts, red socks
2nd strip: Blue shirts with green trim, green shorts, blue socks
Pitch size: 116 x 77 yards
Ground Capacity: 31,000

HONOURS
League Champions: 1977–78 (1)
FA Cup Winners: 1898, 1959 (2)
League Cup Winners: 1978, 1979, 1989, 1990 (4)
European Cup Winners: 1979, 1980 (2)
European Super Cup Winners: 1980 (1)

PREMIERSHIP PERFORMANCE 1994–95

P	W	D	L	F	A	GD	Pts	Pos
42	22	11	9	72	43	+29	77	3rd

Leading Scorer: Stan Collymore (22)
Highest Attendance: 28,882

NOTTINGHAM FOREST

QUEENS PARK RANGERS

Rangers Stadium, South Africa Road, London, W12 7PA. Telephone: 0181-743 0262. Fax: 0181-749 0994
Chairman: R.C. Thompson
Manager: Ray Wilkins
Youth Development Officer: C.P. Gieler
Sponsors: Compaq
Nickname: 'Rangers'
Colours: Blue and white hooped shirts, white shorts, white socks
2nd strip: All red with black trim
Pitch size: 112 x 72 yards
Ground Capacity: 19,200

HONOURS
League Cup Winners: 1967 (1)

PREMIERSHIP PERFORMANCE 1994–95

P	W	D	L	F	A	GD	Pts	Pos
42	17	9	16	61	59	+2	60	8th

Leading Scorer: Les Ferdinand (24)
Highest Attendance: 18,948

Hillsborough, Sheffield, S6 1SW. Telephone: 01742 343122. Fax: 01742 337145
Chairman: D.G. Richards
Team Manager: David Pleat
Youth Development Officer: C. Baker
Sponsors: Sanderson Electronics
Nickname: 'The Owls'
Colours: Blue & white striped shirts, blue shorts, blue/white socks
2nd strip: All black with yellow trim
Pitch size: 115 x 77 yards
Ground Capacity: 36,020

HONOURS
League Champions: 1902–03, 1903–04, 1928–29, 1929–30 (4)
FA Cup Winners: 1896, 1907, 1935 (3)
League Cup Winners: 1991 (1)
Charity Shield Winners: 1935 (1)

PREMIERSHIP PERFORMANCE 1994–95

P	W	D	L	F	A	GD	Pts	Pos
42	13	12	17	49	57	-8	51	13th

Leading Scorer: Mark Bright (11)
Highest Attendance: 34,051

SHEFFIELD WEDNESDAY

The Dell, Milton Road, Southampton, SO9 4XX. Telephone: 01703 220505. Fax: 01703 330360.
Chairman: F.G.L. Askham
Team Manager: Alan Ball
Youth Development Officer: S. Henderson
Sponsors: Dimplex (UK) Ltd
Nickname: 'The Saints'
Colours: Red and white striped shirts, black shorts, black socks with red/white trim
2nd strip: Light blue shirts with royal blue stripe, light blue shorts, royal blue socks turquoise trim
Pitch size: 110 x 72 yards
Ground Capacity: 15,000

SOUTHAMPTON

HONOURS
FA Cup Winners: 1976 (1)

PREMIERSHIP PERFORMANCE 1994–95

P	W	D	L	F	A	GD	Pts	Pos
42	12	18	12	61	63	-2	54	10th

Leading Scorer: Matthew Le Tissier (20)
Highest Attendance: 15,210

TOTTENHAM HOTSPUR

White Hart Lane, 748 High Road, Tottenham, London, N17 0AP. Telephone: 0181-365 5000. Fax: 0181-365 5005.
Chairman: A.M. Sugar
Manager: Gerry Francis
Youth Development Officer: J. Moncur
Sponsors: Hewlett Packard
Nickname: 'Spurs'
Colours: White shirts, navy shorts, white socks
2nd strip: All navy with purple trim
Pitch size: 110 x 73 yards
Ground Capacity: 33,147

HONOURS
League Champions: 1950–51, 1960–61 (2)
FA Cup Winners: 1901, 1921, 1961, 1962, 1967, 1981, 1982, 1991 (8)
League Cup Winners: 1971, 1973 (2)
Charity Shield Winners: 1920, 1951, 1961, 1962, 1967 – shared, 1991 – shared (6)
European Cup-Winners Cup Winners: 1963 (1)
UEFA Cup Winners: 1972, 1984 (2)

PREMIERSHIP PERFORMANCE 1994–95

P	W	D	L	F	A	GD	Pts	Pos
42	16	14	12	66	58	+8	62	7th

Leading Scorer: Jurgen Klinsmann (20)
Highest Attendance: 33,040

41

WEST HAM UNITED

Boleyn Ground, Green Street, Upton Park, London, E13 9AZ. Telephone: 0181-548 2748. Fax: 0181-548 2758.
Chairman: T.W. Brown
Manager: Harry Redknapp
Youth Development Officer: J. Hampson
Sponsors: Dagenham Motors
Nickname: 'The Hammers'
Colours: Claret shirts with blue sleeves, white shorts, white socks with claret/blue trim
2nd strip: Blue shirts with two claret hoops, blue shorts, blue socks
Pitch size: 112 x 72 yards
Ground Capacity: 26,000

HONOURS
FA Cup Winners: 1964, 1975, 1980 (3)
Charity Shield Winners: 1964 – shared (1)
European Cup-Winners Cup' Winners: 1965 (1)

PREMIERSHIP PERFORMANCE 1994–95

P	W	D	L	F	A	GD	Pts	Pos
42	13	11	18	44	48	-4	50	14th

Leading Scorer: Tony Cottee (13)
Highest Attendance: 24,783

Selhurst Park Ground, London, SE25 6PY. Telephone: 0181-771 2233. Fax: 0181-768 0640.
Chairman: S.G. Reed
Team Manager: Joe Kinnear
Youth Development Officer: R. Smith
Sponsors: Elonex Computers
Nickname: 'The Dons'
Colours: All navy blue with yellow trim
2nd strip: All white with black trim
Pitch Size: 110 x 74 yards
Ground Capacity: 18,300

HONOURS
FA Cup Winners: 1988 (1)

PREMIERSHIP PERFORMANCE 1994–95

P	W	D	L	F	A	GD	Pts	Pos
42	15	11	16	48	65	-17	56	9th

Leading Scorer: Efan Ekoku (9)
Highest Attendance: 18,224

WIMBLEDON

PREMIERSHIP COMPETITION!

WIN A MITRE ULTIMA FOOTBALL

Where did Jurgen go?

All you have to do is answer these three simple questions:

1. Which player/manager led Middlesbrough to promotion last season?

2. Who was the Premiership's leading scorer in 1994-95?

3. Which club did Jurgen Klinsmann join at the end of the 1994-95 season?

Send your completed entry form to:
Premier League Competition
Grandreams Ltd, Jadwin House, 205/211 Kentish Town Road,
London NW5 2JU.

Closing date for entries is Thursday 29th February 1996.
Don't forget to include your name, age and address.

A Mitre Ultima football will be awarded to the sender of the first correct entry drawn out of the bag on the closing date. The senders of the second and third correct entries will each receive Umbro and Highgrove Stationery products. The publisher's decision is final, and no correspondence will be entered into.

PREMIER LEAGUE COMPETITION

Answers:

1..

2..

3..

Name...Age......

Address...

....

....

Post code...

43

SOCCER RECORDS

YEAR	CHAMPIONS	YEAR	CHAMPIONS	YEAR	CHAMPIONS
1888-89	Preston North End	1924-25	Huddersfield Town	1962-63	Everton
1889-90	Preston North End	1925-26	Huddersfield Town	1963-64	Liverpool
1890-91	Everton	1926-27	Newcastle United	1964-65	Manchester United
1891-92	Sunderland	1927-28	Everton	1965-66	Liverpool
1892-93	Sunderland	1928-29	Sheffield Wednesday	1966-67	Manchester United
1893-94	Aston Villa	1929-30	Sheffield Wednesday	1967-68	Manchester City
1894-95	Sunderland	1930-31	Arsenal	1968-69	Leeds United
1895-96	Aston Villa	1931-32	Everton	1969-70	Everton
1896-97	Aston Villa	1932-33	Arsenal	1970-71	Arsenal
1897-98	Sheffield United	1933-34	Arsenal	1971-72	Derby County
1898-99	Aston Villa	1934-35	Arsenal	1972-73	Liverpool
1899-1900	Aston Villa	1935-36	Sunderland	1973-74	Leeds United
1900-01	Liverpool	1936-37	Manchester City	1974-75	Derby County
1901-02	Sunderland	1937-38	Arsenal	1975-76	Liverpool
1902-03	The Wednesday	1938-39	Everton	1976-77	Liverpool
1903-04	The Wednesday	1946-47	Liverpool	1977-78	Nottingham Forest
1904-05	Newcastle United	1947-48	Arsenal	1978-79	Liverpool
1905-06	Liverpool	1948-49	Portsmouth	1979-80	Liverpool
1906-07	Newcastle United	1949-50	Portsmouth	1980-81	Aston Villa
1907-08	Manchester United	1950-51	Tottenham Hotspur	1981-82	Liverpool
1908-09	Newcastle United	1951-52	Manchester United	1982-83	Liverpool
1909-10	Aston Villa	1952-53	Arsenal	1983-84	Liverpool
1910-11	Manchester United	1953-54	Wolverhampton Wanderers	1984-85	Everton
1911-12	Blackburn Rovers			1985-86	Liverpool
1912-13	Sunderland	1954-55	Chelsea	1986-87	Everton
1913-14	Blackburn Rovers	1955-56	Manchester United	1987-88	Liverpool
1914-15	Everton	1956-57	Manchester United	1988-89	Arsenal
1919-20	West Bromwich Albion	1957-58	Wolverhampton Wanderers	1989-90	Liverpool
1920-21	Burnley	1958-59	Wolverhampton Wanderers	1990-91	Arsenal
1921-22	Liverpool	1959-60	Burnley	1991-92	Leeds United
1922-23	Liverpool	1960-61	Tottenham Hotspur		
1923-24	Huddersfield Town	1961-62	Ipswich Town		

PREMIER LEAGUE

YEAR	CHAMPIONS
1992-93	Manchester United
1993-94	Manchester United
1994-95	Blackburn Rovers

YEAR	LEAGUE CUP WINNERS	YEAR	LEAGUE CUP WINNERS	YEAR	LEAGUE CUP WINNERS
1960-61	Aston Villa	1972-73	Tottenham Hotspur	1984-85	Norwich City
1961-62	Norwich City	1973-74	Wolverhampton W.	1985-86	Oxford United
1962-63	Birmingham City	1974-75	Aston Villa	1986-87	Arsenal
1963-64	Leicester City	1975-76	Manchester City	1987-88	Luton Town
1964-65	Chelsea	1976-77	Aston Villa	1988-89	Nottingham Forest
1965-66	West Bromwich Albion	1977-78	Nottingham Forest	1989-90	Nottingham Forest
1966-67	QPR	1978-79	Nottingham Forest	1990-91	Sheffield Wednesday
1967-68	Leeds United	1979-80	Wolverhampton W.	1991-92	Manchester United
1968-69	Swindon Town	1980-81	Liverpool	1992-93	Arsenal
1969-70	Manchester City	1981-82	Liverpool	1993-94	Aston Villa
1970-71	Tottenham Hotspur	1982-83	Liverpool	1994-95	Liverpool
1971-72	Stoke City	1983-84	Liverpool		

YEAR	FA CUP WINNERS	YEAR	FA CUP WINNERS	YEAR	FA CUP WINNERS
1872	Wanderers	1910-11	Bradford City	1958-59	Nottingham Forest
1873	Wanderers	1911-12	Barnsley	1959-60	Wolverhampton Wanderers
1874	Oxford University	1912-13	Aston Villa	1960-61	Tottenham Hotspur
1875	Royal Engineers	1913-14	Burnley	1961-62	Tottenham Hotspur
1876	Wanderers	1914-15	Sheffield United	1962-63	Manchester United
1877	Wanderers	1919-20	Aston Villa	1963-64	West Ham United
1878	Wanderers	1920-21	Tottenham Hotspur	1964-65	Liverpool
1879	Old Etonians	1921-22	Huddersfield Town	1965-66	Everton
1880	Clapham Rovers	1922-23	Bolton Wanderers	1966-67	Tottenham Hotspur
1881	Old Carthusians	1923-24	Newcastle United	1967-68	West Bromwich Albion
1882	Old Etonians	1924-25	Sheffield United	1968-69	Manchester City
1883	Blackburn Olympic	1925-26	Bolton Wanderers	1969-70	Chelsea
1884	Blackburn Rovers	1926-27	Cardiff City	1970-71	Arsenal
1885	Blackburn Rovers	1927-28	Blackburn Rovers	1971-72	Leeds United
1886	Blackburn Rovers	1928-29	Bolton Wanderers	1972-73	Sunderland
1887	Aston Villa	1929-30	Arsenal	1973-74	Liverpool
1888	West Bromich Albion	1930-31	West Bromwich Albion	1974-75	West Ham United
1888-89	Preston North End	1931-32	Newcastle United	1975-76	Southampton
1889-90	Blackburn Rovers	1932-33	Everton	1976-77	Manchester United
1890-91	Blackburn Rovers	1933-34	Manchester City	1977-78	Ipswich Town
1891-92	West Bromwich Albion	1934-35	Sheffield Wednesday	1978-79	Arsenal
1892-93	Wolverhampton Wanderers	1935-36	Arsenal	1979-80	West Ham United
1893-94	Notts County	1936-37	Sunderland	1980-81	Tottenham Hotspur
1894-95	Aston Villa	1937-38	Preston North End	1981-82	Tottenham Hotspur
1895-96	Sheffield Wednesday	1938-39	Portsmouth	1982-83	Manchester United
1896-97	Aston Villa	1946	Derby County	1983-84	Everton
1897-98	Nottingham Forest	1946-47	Charlton Athletic	1984-85	Manchester United
1898-99	Sheffield United	1947-48	Manchester United	1985-86	Liverpool
1899-1900	Bury	1948-49	Wolverhampton Wanderers	1986-87	Coventry City
1900-01	Tottenham Hotspur	1949-50	Arsenal	1987-88	Wimbledon
1901-02	Sheffield United	1950-51	Newcastle United	1988-89	Liverpool
1902-03	Bury	1951-52	Newcastle United	1989-90	Manchester United
1903-04	Manchester City	1952-53	Blackpool	1990-91	Tottenham Hotspur
1904-05	Aston Villa	1953-54	West Bromwich Albion	1991-92	Liverpool
1905-06	Everton	1954-55	Newcastle United	1992-93	Arsenal
1906-07	Sheffield Wednesday	1955-56	Manchester City	1993-94	Manchester United
1907-08	Wolverhampton Wanderers	1956-57	Aston Villa	1994-95	Everton
1908-09	Manchester United	1957-58	Bolton Wanderers		
1909-10	Newcastle United				

CHAMPIONSHIP WINNERS

18 – Liverpool

10 – Arsenal

9 – Everton, Manchester United

7 – Aston Villa

6 – Sunderland

4 – Newcastle United, Sheffield Wednesday

3 – Blackburn Rovers, Huddersfield Town, Leeds United, Wolverhampton Wanderers

2 – Burnley, Derby County, Manchester City, Portsmouth, Preston North End, Tottenham Hotspur

1 – Chelsea, Ipswich Town, Nottingham Forest, Sheffield United, West Bromwich Albion

FA CUP WINNERS

8 – Manchester United, Tottenham Hotspur

7 – Aston Villa

6 – Arsenal, Blackburn Rovers, Newcastle United

5 – Everton, Liverpool, The Wanderers, West Bromwich Albion

4 – Bolton Wanderers, Manchester City, Sheffield United, Wolverhampton Wanderers

3 – Sheffield Wednesday, West Ham United,

2 – Bury, Nottingham Forest, Old Etonians, Preston North End, Sunderland

1 – Barnsley, Blackburn Olympic, Blackpool, Bradford City, Burnley, Cardiff City, Charlton Athletic, Chelsea, Clapham Rovers, Coventry City, Derby County, Huddersfield Town, Ipswich Town, Leeds United, Notts County, Old Carthusians, Oxford University, Portsmouth, Royal Engineers, Southampton, Wimbledon

LEAGUE CUP WINS

5 – Liverpool

4 – Aston Villa, Nottingham Forest

2 – Arsenal, Manchester City, Norwich City, Tottenham Hotspur, Wolverhampton Wanderers

1 – Birmingham City, Chelsea, Leeds United, Leicester City, Luton Town, Manchester United, Oxford United, QPR, Sheffield Wednesday, Stoke City, Swindon Town, West Bromwich Albion